THE PRIC

THE PRICE OF GOLD

Poems about the Honey Bee

Edited by Joy Howard

Illustrations: Cathy Benson

First published in 2012 by Grey Hen Press
PO Box 450
Keighley
West Yorkshire
BD22 9WS
www.greyhenpress.com

ISBN 978-0-9552952-7-0

Printed by Flexpress Ltd, Birstall, Leicester LE4 3BY

For beekeepers and honey-lovers everywhere ...

and for Doris –
who loves bees.

With all our love

Headleigh Stuart

xx

2·1·2015

...a little, profound, and complicated existence.

Maurice Maeterlinck: The Life of the Bee

Preface

Everyone by now surely knows that there is a crisis in the world bee population. The purpose of this book is not to raise awareness of the situation but to celebrate what it is that honey bees mean for us individually – what we have observed, what we have absorbed from history, myth, legend and literature, what we love. The human relationship with bees goes back to our beginnings, and is deep and universal. But however familiar the territory, there is nothing ordinary about our personal reactions to bees: to their presence in our lives and to the stories that have been woven around them.

Joy Howard

Contents

The Mother Hive

For deep memory, we must learn
the language of bees, investigate hive-life –
how winged atoms make honey and store-cells,
how wax will only generate when the wax-makers
lie together for hours, quiescent, in great heat.

Comb-building takes place at night
at the borders of language and dream,
when the dead come back to talk.
Sometimes memory's partitions melt,
we get to uncover bricked-up fireplaces.

We have a need to remember what is lost,
find it hard to fly the crowded hive,
leave it all behind.
When a store-cell opens,
wild hope bends an ear.

Rose Cook

Migrant Workers

They arrived under cover of darkness.
I saw them when I went out in the morning
To call the gimmers down into the intake.
Their wooden shacks are parked in groups of four
Under the shelter of the old stone wall.

Their open doors face north, south, east and west
And forth they come, humming the usual tune
As sunshine burnishes their uniforms
And warms them as they rise, a living stream
Pouring over the wall onto the heather.

They turn up every year, the migrant workers;
Workers from further south, carrying out
The task set by their masters. Giddy gangs,
Sucking the best from this great fragrant crop.
Seasonal visitors, bringing the harvest home.

Ann Drysdale

The Beekeeper

At weekends, he pretended to hang his own skin
behind the kitchen door. *No use with bees,*
he'd tease and disappear. For years we'd lose
him then; on still summer days a shadow figure
magnified on the whitewashed wall was all we knew.

But as we grew, we learned more of his magic.
Followed unbidden the curls of acrid smoke
to watch, open-mouthed as he calmed the fizzing bees
to a gentle hum, raising the domed roof of the lid.
Inching forward, we hid and held our breath.

Years later, visiting him, only a short walk from death,
his ill-fitting paper-thin fingers holding mine,
I remembered how he had looked back then, as,
turning, he held out a gloved hand covered with bees
for us to see something of the tenacity of love.

His hands danced in and out of shadow
in the dappled light, under the trees, working
an invisible alchemy of their own.

Ann Williams

Swarm

First the seethe round the lowest branch
by the field-side hedge
then the thrum like a purring
like a well-loved slick machine
throbbing throughout my head
and I draw closer close enough
to see the big tawny globe
a few stragglers still arriving
the pulsing   the living kaleidoscope
gold-brown patterning and re-patterning
so I would like to sit on this log
and watch for as long as it takes
for them to achieve their purpose

Gina Shaw

Golden

A Sunday in June
no bees in sight but listen
to the tree humming

Eleanor Livingstone

4

Weather Watch

The bees, back to the wall,
wait for blusters to stop,
rain showers to move with the clouds,

building in secret, larders,
worker and queen cells
until blue skies resume.

I wait for the sun to come,
for morning to warm and thicken.
I will ravage those bees,

rehouse half in a parallel hive,
divide their reserves,
victuals and populace.

The queen thinks she has done
the rushing out, the swarm,
the big upheaval, relocation

from high in a tree
by a bee-line to chosen refuge,
old wall in the woods.

If I can contain them,
they are my bees,
otherwise wild nature's.

Here are my veil and gloves
to manoeuvre my adversaries,
tomorrow's friends.

Sally Evans

Sayah Çam Bali

Time spent in Turkish forests, on the way to Kusadasi
eating black pine honey watching women dyeing cloth
weaving at their looms in Kovanlik Kayu. The first time
you heard the muezzin call from the minaret in Mugla
his voice stretching like syrup across the Menderes Plain.
The time you spoke with the old man at the roadside
his wife stitching lace that now graces your table.

It was from the old man you learned that pine honey, *sayah
çam bali,* wasn't honey at all, but honeydew, sap spat from scale
insects that gathered the honey, that turned it to dew
that bees collect to make their honey. From him you learned
the Turkish pine is called *pinus brutia,* its bark reddish-orange
its needles green-yellow, cones hard and heavy, that the eucalyptus
trees lining the road across the marshes were planted to drain

water, that they drink so many gallons each day – how many?
How many? When you left the old man and his wife below
the scent of pines and diesel, oleander and oregano, it was time
for their ablutions in the spring at the roadside, trickling down
from the Çubukbeli Pass. Time for cleansing. Time for prayer.
Old man facing east, his wife hands folded, calm as paint. In my
hands a jar of blackgold – dew drawn from phloem by insect jaws.

Geraldine Green

6

White Bees
(Aberdeen Bestiary, 12th C)

The hives, three cones
pull in their lines of bees.
A vertical dive.

Staring upside-down ghosts,
bald as maggots, fall dizzily
then swivel, zoom
right-angled to the open mouth.

Shrouded baby angels
home into their ribbed bell.

A hum fades and dies
in the painted sky.

Jo Peters

The Bees, Canto Four: Honey
verses i–x

It is as great a miracle for bees to live through winter
   as if we entertained a second life
   after our end in this one. Could we enter

new warmth after that last calamity, the reaper's knife?
   How can the bees know spring will come, when snow
   turns all their world into a woodcut; strife

between extremes, black and white, fire and water, yes and no,
   the same two options that permit computers
   to work so fast, where we would be so slow.

We thrive on in-betweens. We hesitate, we are transmuters
   of black and white to colours, which we love.
   Sleep and distraction are our trouble-shooters.

But bees don't hibernate when winter steals the scene above,
   or bide away in singles like the wasps,
   their cousins and their enemies. They shove

their fellows round in circles, fan their wings, emitting gasps
   and strenuously work up such a heat
   as saves them in their crisis. Then the clasps

on honey cells are broken, and delightedly they eat.
   Were not the honey gathered in and stored,
   the summer bees our yearly garden treat,

there'd be no honey in our supermarkets to afford
   and none at village shops, the local kind,
   from daisies, gorse and broom, or local hoard

of clover, wallflower, heather, sage and sycamore combined.
   The cloudy, white or golden kind, the runny
   syrupy red or bracken gold, aligned

in sparkling pots of glass, with swirling labels. How much money
   would be too much? We buy, and bear it home
   into our kitchen making it more sunny.

Sally Evans

The Girls in the Miellerie

Their perfume clings to you as you waver
between racks of gold, the crosshatched furls
of candles, handwarm wax slabs, opaque cakes

of soap. All day they stand among this,
guardians of a shrine to honey
and honey-drenched, breathing sugar, melting

beneath crisp shirts. They proffer spatulas dipped
and dripping; you thrust out your tongue to catch
the glistening strands, your chin stuck

with pearls, your bared teeth gritty – savouring
the liquid fall of hair, the grain of blond skin
as they lean towards you; they can offer you

anything, from the bitter dark of chestnut or pine
to the cream of the smallest blooms. And you know
how the bee feels, stumbling from flower

to flower, hardly able to choose which open throat
to bury itself in. Leaving heavy, drunk,
bags full to overflowing with the sweet stuff.

Caroline Price

Out of Season

Honeycomb weighted with nectar
of local flowers,
meadowsweet, campion, clover,
infusions from
dog-rose and vetch.

Its wafer of wax is round
as if for communion,
we take it
reverently on the tongue.

This winter,
outside there are stings,
snow-swarms,
flakes fierce as white bees,

and we
are golden-throated,
spoon long sugars of stopped sun.

Isobel Thrilling

Honeysuckle

I drowse in the warmth of velvet skin
and wake to eyes deep brimming
I sway to the gentle weight of your limbs
while you brush my face with bee's wing hands
and bring me back to the morning

Take me to your humming hive
and make me honey
a golden drop of sun to thrive
in a secret scented cell
alive
for winter's coming

Joy Howard

The Beekeeper's Boy

He refused the veil, would flaunt himself bare
faced and necked before the hive, fix on gloves,
then, staring as a man stares at the horse he loves,
with his slow croon seduce them through the air,
his hands rotating as a man moulds dough.

At first a cloud of black specks, quick rustling
like a forest in spate, then the shapes
began: wheels, spirals, plumes, swags of grapes,
apes on masts, lions tracking, snails tussling,
stags locking, death's heads, then a rainbow

as colour changed line with the fast or slow
beating of wings: yellow, red, amber,
sage green, the year's leaf palate of trees
vaulted in air, while the sugared noise of bees
surged and fell in a restless ecstatic purr.

The village never thought well of him though;
bees swarm: he just exploited it. No one
blinked when late October they found the hive
empty, him in the pond scarcely alive.
Some skills are too flimsy to build a life upon.

Marianne Burton

Figures of Eight

You were late, you told me
but smiling, without apology,
because you'd been working with the *petits insectes*

you'd inherited from your father-in-law,
you'd not known anything about bees before

but now you loved them,
now you saw them everywhere –
there are bees wherever you look, you said,
even on the rooftops of Paris! –

Yes, anyone gazing down on the city
would see roof gardens, balconies
dotted with hives; Paris in spring

is not just for lovers
but for bees finding food like lovers
as snowdrop, coltsfoot and willow break into flower,

a softening, a filling out
of the palest cream until green
dusts the sky, the temperature rising by a few degrees

and the sun high enough to finger
mansards and high windows,
the sleepers unhuddling
and venturing out, drowsy from overwintering,

climbing from the darkness of yards and stairwells
into the open, their other lives
as invisible below

as the traffic is inaudible; all they can hear
is humming, bees freighting the air
with their sweet trajectories.

Caroline Price

13

An Ordinary Walk

in an ordinary wood (the one
behind their house)
goes one step awry

into a wild bees' nest
and now she knows
nothing – not where she is
who she is
how old she is (five)

only that
her hair hums
branches crackle
a smoke of bees
spiralling.

Like a queen
swollen with eggs
her throat bloats
She sings silent high Bs
dances the body electric

Sealed in her
raw skin pullulating
with tiny soldering irons
she hatches
a new self: a hive

of allergy. Since then
honey fevers her
she is inflamed by candles
imperilled by Pledge.
She could die of spring.

She knows now
there are no
ordinary woods.

Stevie Krayer

Cure for Bee Stings

Great Aunt Mollie lived
as her mother had
in a cabin of chestnut logs
with a roof of oak shingles.
Her bedstead was corded with ropes,
a mattress stuffed with rye straw.
She made soap of hogfat
and hickory ashes cooked in a kettle.
She had five cures for bee stings.

Slightly moist sugar cube
applied to welt,
a paste of baking soda,
slices of raw onion,
poultice of summer savory,
dolly blue

She prepared the hive for winter:
black tar paper wrapped round
the wood at the base to deter mice.
Her tools were a lantern, a knife
and a syrup can.
Wild honeycombs hung from her rafters,
pointed at the base, rounded on top,
the bees huddled in the centre combs
to keep warm.

Great Uncle Edward preferred
a paste of baking soda, vinegar
and water or tobacco juice or
his home-made toothpaste.
I liked a copper penny taped
to the wound as I could spend it after.

Edward was away trading beaver pelt,
Mollie in the middle of making cornbread
when the stroke took her.
She'd just gathered a jar
of tiny wood asters.
Edward came
and we forced the bees
out of their hive
so they could aid
the ascent of her soul.

Margaret Speak

February

A watery moon blinks through storm clouds,
eyeing the white ground with suspicion.

A sign that winter is passing,
as surely as the swallows, still a world away,
watch the shadows lengthen,

swarm in a tepid sky,
grow sleek, remember distance.

Inside the hive – silence.
A furry mass of bodies – tiny throb of stilled life,
the temperature of mid-summer.

Ann Williams

Customs

In Ljubljana the Sunday market stalls
are golden with sunshine and honey.
Keeping to the shady side, mindful
of hand luggage limitations, I buy
scented candles shaped like flowers

and beehives each with a wax bee
stuck to one side. In small jars
apricots swim in less than 100mls
of honey sweet Slovenian liqueur.
I browse from stall to stall.

Fat ripe pears float in rows
suspended in honeyed brandy
like grotesque medical specimens.
A sign explains how bottles
are fitted around the infant pears

which grow inside their own
individual glasshouses
still attached to the tree.
I leave the market, my bag filled
with wax bees ready to fly.

Eleanor Livingstone

Dancing

when bees wake after their long slow overcoat of snow
warms and splits into two pieces
slides sideways from the hive   like a discarded blanket

when the first scouts come and re-explore the garden
begin the dance that says
there's nectar to be found among primroses

I   standing at the window
sensing new messages in the pulse of the morning
the secret hum of the world

turn and see you kneeling on the floor
gathering our granddaughter's toys   putting them back
in what passes for order in our clumsy lives

                        and I open the window

because that's what we have to do each spring
send out the scouts   ask the right questions
wonder how   after so many years

I still lay our breakfast table the same way
eat the same treats of porridge with honey
treasure days   when you come in dancing

Caroline Carver

19

Honey/ Honig

I stand gasping inside the cloy of black netting,
sucking in the sweet smoke – as much to try
to calm myself, as drowse them. And they crawl
in front of my myopia, black-hair legs poking
through the mesh. Then stare their compound image
of me back into the mind of the hives. And they calm me.
I become soporific, tuning into their insect leg-language,
the cleaning of their antennae, their modulating rhythms
of humbuzz.

I never take much of their honey. Dad grumbles
about the falling yield – talks about 'setting a fire
under the buggers'. So I've taken to hobbling into Lidl
– to check out offers on runny honey. Back
in the jarring-shed, the cool brick all around me
blooming with rings of white salts, I am magician.
Our yield climbs up the shining jars, as I mix
the German bees' Honig with our Norfolk's
– ours so much yellower, so much like the sunshine
that pushes in through the cobwebbed window.

I often wonder if our bees ever get fed up
with the taste of rape.

Char March

20

Ellemford

I heard them before I saw them – heard it,
a strange organ playing warm chords
of pristine thirds, vertical stacks of harmony,
as if the breath of the just-hatched summer
blew through the pipes.

Around the corner, I saw it – a sweet froth of petals,
just one tree in bloom against a canvas of green,
the pink and white of apple blossom making candy floss
on the serious brown trunk of the tree.

And mists and swathes of dark bodies,
weaving a weft of sound
around the still warp of branches.
Small ministers in collars of amber fur,
murmuring sermons of ecstasy.
No starched white here, just skin-soft petals,
their pinkness blushing in the sun's heat.

The whole tree pulsed
with a singing, sobbing rhythm
that called to places deeper than the tree roots.
It must have touched the bedrock,
this chorus of pleasure, thousands of wings
driving the air into waves of sound
that crashed and rolled together
like a rising sea.

That moment, the grass sang, the earth sang,
the sky rang with the wordless music
of beings bringing together what was separate.
The world turned slow in a spell of amazement
which, later, would swell into fruit.
And the sun dripped down golden over everything,
like honey from above.
Like blessings.

Fiona Durance

21

Honeycomb

It is too beautiful to eat.
Knife crumbles it from gold to dark.
Our keenest edge cannot stay sharp
while in our walls, which seemed so strong,
damp murmurs with the evening sleet.
I wonder if I live too long

but then I taste the honeycomb,
its waxen white upon my teeth,
its liquid sun which hides beneath.
Small deities, of wind or moon,
behold me. In my shabby room
I am a god. I lick the spoon.

Alison Brackenbury

Blue

I remember all those summers –
straw grass, the ground rock hard,
bees in the lavender –

and now, tonight, I sit here,
hot, impatient, terrified
by all the disappearing years

and unaware of anything
except this long estrangement
from my shrinking life,

until I hear the hum of bees
below my window, come to make
more honey in my sour heart's hive.

J A Priestman

Alone

In ancient role she shares her news.
Deaf, they carry on making honey.

Pat Simmons

In a Summer Wreathed with Bees

Heath-brushed and orchard bees,
'starline' and 'golden' bees,
   I watch you weave
from vetch to thyme. Listen:
how the rock-rose sings.

Buckfast and Norfolk bees,
you busk through summer,
   a vibrato in heather;
the drowsy leaves are
basking in your sound.

Honeybees: ever-hum.
Accomplices of wind
   and sun. You glide
through ciphers, u.v. lines
on bell and stem.

Feral bees in chestnut furs,
black-haired bees
   on northern moors,
coal-dipped and dwindling.
We thrive: you fall –

in dreams, I try to call you –
I hear your songs grow
   hesitant and thin.
The world you gave us
teeters on your wings.

Lynne Wycherley

May Swarm

A swag of humming fur in a summer tree
mini-harmonicas thrumming a bass note
the whole ensemble
hanging like alien fruit.

There in the afternoon sun
it sways a little
and hums. A few stragglers
dither outside, then settle.

Hidden under heaving pelts
the queen draws them, sure
as iron files to a magnet
deep in the core.

Let her escape they'll rise
a black and amber cloud,
striped ballerinas pirouetting air
their little daggers clenched
between honeyed thighs.

A C Clarke

At Buckfast Abbey
(in memory)

Stone by grey stone rising,
bones of praise. Transepts
and nave. A tall shape
by the lour of the moor,
its rood-screens of rain.

Benedictine, husked in black,
they cleave themselves
to the Rule. Obedience.
Poverty. Chastity. Each day
he takes the veil, walks

to a wedding. Brother Adam,
keeper of the bees, whose
once-young hands were stung
with torments, a dress of salt
and onion-juice on his skin.

Age twenty, how he trembled
when the first swarm rose
and sang. Freed from a skep,
it busied its seeds on burlap,
hung its storm from a tree.

Now his hands glide, practised
as a lover, on the crowded
lattice, the river of the bees.
Gentled to peace, a thrum
of intercession in their wings.

Sun-gatherers, they fizz their atoms,
scent the wick his litanies
will rise on. With heather,
dogwood, red clover,
transubstantiations of summer.

He stoops to the queen. Sunk
in her tracery, brooding her dream.
Our Lady. At night the brothers
pace their bounded rooms.
She beds in gold, her tomb.

Apis mellifera: even the name
speaks honey, easing the iron
of the Rule. Soft wax, sweet wine.
He lifts a comb: his dark eyes
read its amber light and shine.

Lynne Wycherley

A *Gift of Bees*

*'...a hive of bees...sent in your name to provide years of harvest
for a landless person'*

You sent a dream – of bees packed down in winter,
a furred vibration, wings and feet tight-
milling: the ticklish passage to the centre,
a moment's audience with the queen's heart
whispering, then exile to the far rim
where lives dwindle. Time slows. The sweet
comb thins. But now! – feel this! – the stream
of warmth, the dance of scents! – and up and out
they burst, the foragers, trample and dredge
their feet in gold powder, plunge curled
tongues in sticky cups, load their thighs
until they sway and tremble on the edge
of see-sawing petals. Hear their humming rise
to a shout, as they pollinate the world.

Christine Webb

Secret Weapon

Bees could be used to detect chemical weapons, but only if government funding is increased to stop their decline. (News item, 2008)

Don't grab. Just watch them. And Ollie watches
in that holy attention of being two years old.
Honey bees are raiding the potentilla hedge
scouring its yellow faces clean of pollen
buzzing a fuschia bush into a tremble of scarlet bells
dive-bombing purple spires of buddleia.

However is the government going to break the news
put the offer on the table; tell the bees
that resources will be available
to help them survive...But only if they agree
to be our Number One Secret Weapon.
And how will the training schedule be managed?

No... don't tell me. I can see it. Agent 15 (BZ)
that incapacitating little number
injected into the sprawling mallow by the shed
each candy-pink flower full of it.

And roses. They'd be good.
Densely packed petals, bursting with velvet fragrance...
Could hide a multitude. Our bees would soon get the hang
of sniffing out the nasties.

And will all the bees be needed
or can some be spared for traditional duties?
Will it be a phased withdrawal of world pollination
or a short sharp shock, I wonder.

And has anybody told Whitehall that the world as we know it
will disappear five years on when there are no more honey bees?
No fruit. No crops. No flowers. No trees.
Maybe we can grow potatoes, though that's doubtful.
They flower too.

Still, we'll be in no danger from chemical weapons.
So that's all right then.
Meanwhile, in my garden, I'm going to make the most
of watching Ollie, watching bees.

Sheila Templeton

Nothing

You open a door in a dog-rose,
honey, and let me in.

You loosen the tongues of clouds,
my bee-keeper, and let me listen.

You take a swarm of bees out of my mouth,
that is your right.

You lead me to you like a stony road
over-looked by the hardiest walker,
a road without house or hive.

You give me nothing, my dear,
but a single tear from our long-lost year,
honey's last will and testament.

Penelope Shuttle

Cargo

We found beeswax on the shore
as we beachcombed
that summer;
threw misshapen lumps
into the burning driftwood;
let them flare
into the sea-wind.

We knew of no wreck
for so strange a cargo;
but dream still
of the black wax
in the bleached wood,
the visitation of salt,
the resinous haze.

How faint the fuel –
the drift
of the dreaming gene –
the precipitation of dead
bearing on their clavicles
bee-necklaces of amber.

Pauline Stainer

Inch of Gold

I was sorry your bees died. Every summer
your envoys have negotiated the slope
between us: the rise of the field's not been
too much for them, the distance within their span.
Somehow my riches of lavender, rosehedge, weeds
have nourished their broods, and stretched
across a half-mile this furry humming line.

We tell bees our deaths, but can't warn them
of the small messenger that carries theirs.
The hives are cold now; the last inch of honey
crystallises. I can't bear to eat
the gold at the bottom of the jar.

Christine Webb

Poorly Bees

Based on Virgil's Georgics, *Book IV, lines 251–276*

They're just the same as we are, really, bees.
They too get sicknesses from time to time
And you can always tell when they're not right.
They lose their colour and their shine, they go
Peaky and thin. Then they bring out their dead
In a long, sad funeral procession.
Some dangle on the threshold by their feet
While others pine inside, hungry and cold.
They make a deeper sound, a drawn-out murmur
Like a cool south wind moaning in the woods,
The troubled mutter of the ebbing tide
Or the way fire growls in a sealed furnace.
As soon as possible, burn fragrant resin
And feed them honey – drip it through reed pipes
So as to encourage them to eat it.
Ground-up oak-apples, rose petals and raisins
Even good wine, boiled down over a flame.
Thyme from the mountainside, strong-smelling centaury
And the boiled roots of the gold-centred, purple
Aster Amellus (the Michaelmas daisy).
Leave these as food, in baskets, at their door.

Ann Drysdale

Hum

The way that honey drops,
in long, languorous pears of gold,
you sense the luxurious weight.

Watch it pool, mound and pool,
all in slow motion, as if it lived
in a different timeframe. Funny,

how something so indolent
should result from the noise and bustle
of hard work. It glows with silence.

A secret light. Born from the hearts
of flowers, translated by bees
into a language of sweetness

that coats the tongue. Like chocolate
but cleaner. Like treacle but lighter.
Like toffee but fluid and cool.

Impervious to mould. Known to be healing.
Voluptuous slink of a half-lidded dream.
Bee potion – drowsy, fragrant, strong.

Fiona Durance

Beeing

When I was bees
we dozed to our hive-hum
 woke to wing-breeze sunshine
     lived for the drunken plunge
          into flower hearts
     gold dusted bumbled back
carried the world in our bent elbows

I left the hive when my feet grew long
and now my toes can reach the earth
     on quiet nights I miss the song
     my back is dull for lack of gilding
now I see my colour
hear my voice

Angela France

Honey Guide

That afternoon we stood in the orchard
under a ceiling of opening flowers –
you'd bought a swarm of bees from Pensilva

On the bliss of their buzzing intensity flowed
a thorough humming
a May song hefting into the hive

You showed me the queen
knew by her soft golden colour
she'd be gentle easy to find With your open
hand urging them forward you walked the bees in

Late afternoon when the last one
trickled over the threshold you took my hand
walked me into your house

and under the waxy candlelit ceiling
your touch on my skin was full of the day
honeyed winged singing

Roz Quillan Chandler

Without Them

In the early morning sunshine
he strides to check his hives,
finds an eerie silence, bees gone,
leaving behind honey, pollen,
fragrant wax, despair,
his livelihood fallen victim
to Colony Collapse Disorder.

Hope is on the wing.
In a white cotton suit
and mesh veil
the beekeeper resumes
his gentle craft.

Bernie Kenny

The Honey Seller, 1800

Under the Castle gate
bringing my stores to the kitchen
I am asked to wait.
Honey shines in crocks in my basket.

The gardener wants to know, he says,
if this is a bee-skep hole.
Can we keep bees in it?
He leads me round the old bowls green,

shows me a stone-cut shallow niche.
Am I expected to explain
this is no bee ledge, but a sconce
for a graven image? Dare I be the one

to point out an older, Catholic custom
where queens and kings, and those before them
followed religions no longer approved?
Time has taught the uses of silence.

I answer: Grassy slopes favour the bees,
clover in fields, thyme in the stones,
the moors of heather and shrub myrtle.
Meanwhile, I would not fetch my subjects here

for they are outside workers, like myself.
I bring their produce to your gate.
The kitchen pays me fairly, then
hands me last time's empty crocks –

He nods. On to your business then, he says.
Today I will not stop to gossip,
but flee downhill in daylight,
back to my far-flung bees.

Sally Evans

Black Bees of Colonsay

If honey could sing
this sweet taste would be
            an anthem,
an oratorio,
a meeting of massed choirs
with voices raised
in praise of bees
on a windswept outpost
            in the western sea.

It would tell
of sheltered hives,
a plethora of wildflowers
            whose names trip
from the tongue like a song.
Primrose, clover, heather,
            hawthorn, thyme –
nectar transformed,
an island's essence
            captured in a jar.

Mavis Gulliver

Rout

All summer we were lulled into a dream
of heat and timelessness. We'd listen
to the bees drone in the honeysuckle,
slept long afternoons, their sound on our skin
and in our blood – and when we woke
the sky was evening, the sun out of sight.
It seemed we'd slept for months,
it seemed we'd slept the seasons round.
Meanwhile the hay was in, summer at its height
the bees were loud and diligent but all the time
our eyes were closed our feet still
and our mouths dumb the light had broken
and the hives were full one day then emptying,
the bees were dying one by one, in twos
and threes, in tens and thousands, colonies;
we don't know how to bring them back
we don't know what we've done.

Jo Haslam

What Is It with the Bees?

I'd often watch bees on the foxgloves,
track them by their muffled buzz
as they visited each bell then span away.
They were obsessed with marjoram,
I've seen them shimmy in the air, a message
sent and understood so more would come.
The pink, bee-heavy flowers, bending with
their weight, were always full of hangers-on.

But now, what is it with the bees?
I planted tubs with lavender to pull them in.
At first they came, then none. I miss them
as I miss the butterflies. They were
my growing-up, the background to
our summer talk; their business, my delight.

Ruth Smith

The Beekeepers (after Bruegel)

Is it priestcraft they carry
in skeps bound with briar,
robed like divines
with visors of wicker?

And which flightpath
do they follow, hooded
against the secret swarm
no slits for eyes?

Pauline Stainer

42

Bee-garden

I have done all I can for bees.

I have failed to keep a straight-edged garden,
encouraged waywardness and self-seeding.
I have studied nectar plants, placing them
in inappropriate places on the lawn
their open faces turning to the sun.
I have made landing places with the spotty throats
of foxgloves and engineered squeeze stiles
from antirrhinums, toadflax and the pea.

I have allowed wilderness to creep
over the hedge; I have banned dahlias,
F1 hybrids, sterile double blooms,
insecticide, green deserts, astra turf,
obsessive autumn tidying, paper bags
on prize blooms. But it was too late.

The bees have gone. Once they filled
our lavender with their factory hum,
leaving with their panniers piled high,
summer days secured and memorised
as a blessing on the tongue.

I have forgotten the shape of bees:
their working drab, each like the other.
How they do not sleep it out on thistle flowers
in flashy underpants like the sybaritic bumble bee.
How the dance that brought them to our garden
was choreographed, precise, mathematical.

The absence of bees is not my doing.
I have done all I can for bees.
Yet somewhere there is an unravelling
that might be our undoing.

Perhaps we have undone too much for bees.

Sue Wood

43

Legacy

Six days after Clara died

I stand encaged in sallow meadow
grass, watch four shrouded figures
case her joint, break the 'sterile zone' tape
across the door and enter
the universe she had preserved
for ninety seven years.

From here I watch them moving

through her tiny rooms,
see cupboard doors arching soft
disclosure, imagine shelves shrinking
back to walls, curtains flapping measured
outrage, stirring settled air.

Their hands are laid

upon the pale wardrobe door.
I shut my eyes, see jars
of steeping rose petals blinking
in the slant arctic sun,
their labels proud, meticulously
dated – some as far back as 2001.

I know they'll find it.

Lines of clinking incantations
shuffle ranks, break their cover
till finally, one ghost holds aloft
its airtight prize, strokes
the dry-edged label till it croaks:

Clara's Fireweed Honey Summer 2017.

And now, released from permafrost,
come thoughts of names like heather,
wandering chickadee, reindeer moss
and fireweed, iris, arctic lupine.
Names we only utter now in song.
They came for that which once was mine:

Alaskan summers fossilised in amber.

Deborah Sloan

Bereft

Something has plundered the bees' nest
at the wall's foot where lichened brick
used to meld into a tangle of moss and ivy:
a ragged tear now bleeds earth over the path.
Bees tread circles on the spilled soil,
wings quivering, shifting grains from place
to place and back again.

Each day I pass, I see them working;
fragments of moss, scatters of dried grass,
pulled in to cover their loss.
They can't fill the space.

The sun has faded bare earth,
shrivelled exposed roots.
Ivy leans over the edge of the hole,
blending into the dusty green
of the bees' repairs.

Angela France

Queen Bess and the Bees

The summer so wet that year
– the masque was cancelled,
the garden abandoned to Thisbe,
honeysuckle left to sprawl along
the wall, pestering a musk rose
or strangling an espalier pear.
The day was all mussed up

yet bejewelled. The fountain
spattered onto white marble
slimy with mildew. Drops
spun, as if on tangled wires,
scattered by breezes in a rush
of lavender netted with drizzle,
threaded by a thrush's song as

the Queen arrives bedecked
in her sumptuous embroidery.
She doesn't linger so gardeners
become desultory. To the joy
of bees who've guzzled borage
and eglantine, and now nuzzle
nettles in neglected corners.

Past its zenith, the year starts
to zigzag down. Bees continue
to forage but their flight paths
grow tangential, exploratory,
as the scent of musk rose trails,
teases the air in secluded arbours
– the Queen might never return.

Hilary J Murray

At the Field's Border

Here is the rape, that golden, outrageous flower,
which is sprayed with poison, yet bees haunt,
which rears and blurs harsh pollen, wide, head-high.
But at its feet, see, last year's crop slips through,
the aubergine, soft purple tufts and crests,
the lost child's hair. The bees will feed there too.

Alison Brackenbury

Telling the Bees

A country custom requires you to tell the bees of a death or birth

A circular saw cutting wedges
of soft spring weather, bees
relentlessly buzz the willow,
a sharp halo of need
around silky buds.

Bees do not fold themselves up
to mourn the unassuageable loss
of summer, but crouched in
a still dark suspension
shot with light, like sun seen
through the blood of frail fingers,
they wait in certainty
of winter, until the spring clock
fires them out again round the sallow.

Crossed skeins of rapid morse
led to a field patched
out of brambles, set
with small crazy bee prefabs,
bricks holding down their lids
against a pilfering wind.
Scattered bloom of cloud
rolled across the turf,
everything turning,
lightside of leaf to dark
grass riffling, a zip undone,
bees locking onto the hive like iron filings.

I told them her name
and the number of years.
God knows where they took it,
spinning planetary music
around the flight path
from hive to tree.

Kate Foley

Near Bardsea

The bees I hear are the ones that
live in two hives made from wood
over the dry stone wall just down
from where the road drops from Bardsea
village and joins the coast road. They,
one side of the wall and I, the other.

I watch them, the bees, as they hum
their way into air into honey, gather the
delicacies of spring, spin their winged
bee-sunned bodies into nectar.

Below the earth worms grow rich and fat
on composting bodies – the badger I saw
last October, shot-down crow, wounded
rabbit its glazed eyes gazing up
to the sun, pulled

into darkness by beetles and worms, then,
through nature's slow, alchemical rhythm
turn into light, become the nettles that hide
the hives, become the nettles that throw
green pollen.

I watch them, the bees, coming and going –
their louvred wooden boxes; one with a blue
lid, the other unpainted.

Geraldine Green

Drone

This yellow flowering bush reverberates.
Its strange sussurant murmuring inside
attracts my curiosity. I stop
and push my head into its central part.
Assembled bees are humming there, engrossed
and business-like, communicating all
their urgency and diligence at work.
I listen there until it seems as though
these bees are thrumming deep inside my head,
vibrating all my brain's lethargic cells.
It wakes me up like caffeine, alcohol,
or drugs. I pull my head out in surprise,
and high on bees, skull buzzing, go to work.

Jenny Morris

Tangential

1 *Don't doubt the intention of the bee*

> Saturday afternoon, the keeper's cleared
> the boxes. The bees, deprived,
> are in no mood for peace. They swarm, unwavering,
> savage a boy passing on his bike;
> screaming, he sways, falls
> to the ground.

Don't underestimate the ceremony of revenge

> The young lad, rushed to hospital,
> couldn't be saved.

> The bees died from the stinging.

2 *Out of the fire*

> A bee, free agent, circles the flowers, no price
> on risk. There, a spider waits,
> traps its visitor – the web's tacky threads bind
> its desperate prey.

> The bee, pollen-laden,
> has been about a normal day's work.

>   I watch it
> inventing itself as warrior, wings dipping,
> legs lashing against the ribbed silky-network;
> feel a foolish sympathy for both
> caught in this dance of survival. The bee
> kick-kicks, unloads sticky yellow pollen

> till the web becomes a net spun golden
> as the sacks empty
> onto the stark frame.

All that richness there for the taking

> Shocked, mesmerised, unable to interfere, I head off –
> an hour later, the bee has gone, leaving behind
> a circle of golden spokes.

Katherine Gallagher

52

A Visit to the Bee Man

The bee man smiles a sweet brown smile as I am introduced.
'My friend has come from England, have the bees been kind?'
The cellar walls are lined with jars and I struggle to translate
'Woodland Honey of the Spring'
'Summer Honey of the Meadow'
'Beside the Lake'.

The bee man unscrews lids and gives us tiny spoons,
sweetness fills my mouth, but something else –
the strong dark taste of pine,
the scent of summer,
bean fields, blossom,
clover.

The bee man turns his soft brown eyes on me,
behind him, slowly carving circles in the air
a solitary bee keeps him company.
'Remember I am a thief' he says
'and I have my keeper.'

I choose three jars and handing me my change,
the bee man bows; offers me a candle –
scented beeswax moulded like a hive.
'From the bees, something
I have to give.'

Outside, blinking, he shakes my hand.
'I tell the bees their honey is gone to England'
and walks away down the garden path
past tall beans and late strawberries.
A golden silence falls,
a bee drifts past.

Liz Woods

The Gift

The bees came one summer, left you
combs full of honey you poured
in six wide necked jars and kept
in the cool of your cellar.

You shaded your eyes to the afternoon glare
as if you might see their black swarm
return; as if they might come
over the still burning fields,

to tell you their stories of healing
and distance, of darkness
and work, and you'd tell them back;
to tell you the sun slipped down in the sea

but yours had already slipped from its moorings;
to tell you your lavender, mullein, blood red
of the poppies; all the strong scents,
sealed in the jars you've not opened yet.

This food doesn't spoil. Its sweetness intensifies
over the years. See how its pale gold
gleams from the shelf; how the hive
still seethes with a secret intelligence.

Jo Haslam

Queen

She hurled her man's grey ashes
into the blue sky, watched them
settle on green grass. Back home
put on her white suit with the veil,
and went to talk to her tawny bees.

How can her silence find its mate
in never-ending hum? What comfort
is there in their dark? What softness
from the glinting wings, the armoured bodies,
the five relentless focused eyes?

Broken, immobile, how find rest
in such relentless busyness?
Cut off, apart, what room is there
for her in such a net of knowing
and doing, where part and whole are one?

The lavender's alive with bees;
orange-legged and laden with life,
they probe and pack. The blue sky throbs.
Indoors she takes off her suit, bakes
bread, spreads honey, eats, alone.

Pat Simmons

Shivering

When I had just begun, my work was menial;
cleaning the house and feeding the little ones.
I was rich with jelly and I blessed them with it,
singing and soothing, singing and soothing.

When my jelly failed I rose to the rank of builder,
crafting the six-sided cells in the crates of the gold.
Then, sent to the door, I would wait to carry the sacrament
From returning merchants who trembled on the threshold.

My singing sister flew far with an escort of drones,
came back alone, humming dreams of a home of her own.
But I had no time to listen, the free-fliers claimed me
and showed me the dance of the seekers, the makings of gold.

And now is the time of frowsting and of feasting,
sharing the sweet from the heart of our hexagon-store.
We cherish our queen with the love in the heat of our bodies,
take turns to crawl to the crust of the ball, and to shiver.

Ann Drysdale

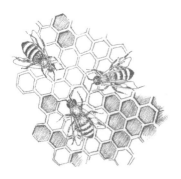

A Perfect Hexagon

It's to the bees' advantage
that the shape providing
the maximum cell area
has the minimum expenditure
in energy and materials.

And engineers confirm
that such a structure provides
the maximum strength –
at 0.05mm thick each wall
supports 25 times
its own weight.

But mathematicians
still conjecture
that as the cell bottom consists
of 3 equal rhombi
there's an isoperimetric
problem for honeycombs –
close to but not quite
the optimal.

Let's hope the bees are working on this.
Time is running out.

Joy Howard

Beewoman

Bulging and pullulating
with fruiting bodies of bees,
the beewoman's hat hums
talkatively. Brimming
with brown, honey-striped
creatures, dripping down
from the rim as slow
as mead, it is less a hat
than a temporary hive;
home to a tribe in transit?

How does she hear her thoughts?
Perhaps her bees
embody them,
active hieroglyphs
charging the white page
of her veil with messages.

As lichen grows into rock
creating soil, so woman
and bees exchange wisdom,
distil into mutual honeycombs
news of a golden citadel
where wealth is stored
against the long attrition
of a sleeping sun.

The beewoman, heavy and awkward
as a ship, dipping with cargo,
is midwife to our fields.
Barren grasses, empty stores
wait the shimmering
tongues of bees.

Kate Foley

Collapsing the Colony

Bees dive into rivers
and ponds, hover on roads
at windscreen height,
find ways into empty buildings.
They're collapsing the colonies;
they won't be stopped.

The bees are anxious.
Their pitch rises in hive and swarm,
in nest and solitary. Bees dancing
at the hive mouth are hesitant,
moving in starts and falters,
lacking an instinct for this.

Workers are sealing eggs in cells
without food, visiting flowers
through habit, returning
with empty legs.

They've carried the world
too long, weathered changes
and changed the weather.
They sense a tipping point
and can do no more.

Angela France

After the Bees

Gold is falling on the honey standard
truck loads of bullion are shipped
from Fort Knox and replaced
by fleece-wrapped jars of liquid amber
(the fabled scents of clover, lavender
jasmine, lost flowers of the past, unreal
as unicorns and dragons, extinct as
butterflies.) The price of vintage
cotton T shirts soars, rarer now
than diamonds; old people tell tales
of crisply laundered cotton sheets
sailing on washing lines, the mythical
coolness of linen, the smell of a fresh
pillow case. Rumours fly of the super-rich
with secret high-walled fields of crops
pollinated by hand: tomatoes, peaches,
mulberry leaves for silk worms,
kept alive by squirrel brushes, slaves
and endless patience. But even they
cannot make honey.

Maggie Butt

60

The Poets

Alison Brackenbury's latest collection is *Singing in the Dark* (Carcanet 2008). She has never kept bees, but always has a cupboardful of honey.

Marianne Burton was awarded a year's mentorship by *Smiths Knoll* and the resulting pamphlet *The Devil's Cut* was a Poetry Book Society Choice; her first full collection is due from Seren in 2012. Her house has a large population of masonry bees.

Maggie Butt is a widely published poet, whose books include *Lipstick* (2007), *petite* (2010) and *Ally Pally Prison Camp* (2011). She is an ex-journalist and BBC Television producer, now Deputy Dean at Middlesex University and Chair of the National Association of Writers in Education. She was once stung by a bumble bee, but still loves honey.

Caroline Carver writes: 'Bees are a marvellously efficient and beautiful link in the eco-system, I've recently seen hives on top of the Vancouver Convention Center, along with lots of suitable wildflowers, as part of its "green roof". Magic.' Caroline is a National prizewinner: her fourth collection will be published by Ward Wood in January 2012.

A C Clarke's pamphlet *A Natural Curiosity* (New Voices Press) came out in 2011. Her third collection, *Fr Meslier's Confession* (Oversteps Books) is due out in 2012. Her partner is addicted to honey – he was allowed *only* one jar a month as a child. She is acutely aware of the current threats to the bee population.

Rose Cook is a bee watcher and lives in Totnes. Originally a member of poetry performance group *Dangerous Cardigans,* she co-founded the popular Totnes poetry and performance forum *One Night Stanza.* She has been published by HappenStance with *Everyday Festival* (2009) and by Oversteps Books who published *Taking Flight* (2009).

Ann Drysdale now lives in South Wales, UK and has been a hill farmer, water-gypsy, newspaper columnist and single parent – not necessarily in that order. Her fifth volume of poetry, *Quaintness and Other Offences* (Cinnamon 2009), has recently joined a mixed list of published writing, including memoir, essays and a gonzo guidebook to the City of Newport.

Fiona Durance has worked in many roles involving communication and pattern – BSL interpreter, dancer, singer, poet coach. She finds bees fascinating, particularly their complex social organisation, geometric building skills and ability to communicate through movement. She also loves Greek thyme honey. Fiona's writing has appeared in many magazines and anthologies.

Sally Evans researched honey bees while writing her poetry book *The Bees* and then began keeping bees as a result. Three years down the line she admires bees even more, but still doesn't understand them. Her other books include *The Honey Seller* and *A Burrell Tapestry*.

Kate Foley divides her time between Amsterdam and Suffolk. Her fifth collection is due out from Shoestring Press in 2012. She is an editor for the magazine *Versal*, has won several prizes and enjoys working with other practising and aspiring poets. She is currently working on a project with Amsterdam Museum on its 'Memory Palace' of collections.

Angela France writes poems, reads poems, studies poems, edits poetry journals and runs a poetry reading series but the day job sometimes gets in the way. Her second collection, *Occupation,* is available from Ragged Raven Press and a pamphlet, *Lessons in Mallemaroking,* was published by Nine Arches Press in 2011.

Katherine Gallagher has five full-length collections of poetry, most recently *Carnival Edge: New & Selected Poems* (Arc Publications 2010), 'its natural territory the exotic and unknown, the fringe and carnivalesque' (*Poetry Review*). 'I've become increasingly interested in bees, a natural wonder of the world. Their importance to our planet is inestimable.'

Geraldine Green has read and been published in the UK, the USA and Italy. Her collections *The Skin* and *Passio* are published by Flarestack, *Poems of a Molecatcher's Daughter* by Palores Publications. *The Other Side of the Bridge* (Indigo Dreams) will be out 2012. She's working on her next collection, *Salt Road*.

Mavis Gulliver's poems focus on the Hebrides. They can be read in magazines, and in the anthology *These Islands We Sing* (Polygon 2011). The honey described in her poem comes from the bees of a tiny island where the air is pure and the nectar is collected from wild flowers.

Jo Haslam has two collections published by Smith/Doorstop. Her work has appeared in poetry magazines such as *The Rialto*, *Ambit* and *The North*. She has also won a number of awards including joint second prize in the 2010 National Poetry Competition. Jo has a small garden planted to attract bees and other wildlife.

Joy Howard lives in West Yorkshire. Poetry has always been part of her life, and after retirement she returned to writing, and founded Grey Hen Press. This is her fifth anthology for Grey Hen and her second collection, *Refurbishment*, was published by Ward Wood in 2011.

Bernie Kenny lives in Dalkey, Co Dublin. She has four collections and her poems have been widely published in magazines. Her translations from the Irish poems of Greagóir Ó Dúill were published in 2005. She believes in the medicinal properties of honey and frequently visits New Zealand, home of prized Manuka honey.

Stevie Krayer has published two poetry collections and a translation of R M Rilke's *The Book of Hours*. She lives in rural west Wales. She is fascinated by bees, and concerned about their future, but finds the taste of honey oddly fails to live up to its PR.

Eleanor Livingstone's first full collection, *Even the Sea* (Red Squirrel Press 2010) was shortlisted for the 2010 London New Poetry award for first collections. Other publications include *The Last King of Fife* (HappenStance 2005) and as editor *Skein of Geese* (The Shed Press 2008). She is the Director of StAnza.

Char March is an award-winning poet, playwright and fiction writer. Her latest poetry collections are *The Thousand Natural Shocks* and *The Cloud Appreciation Society's Day Out*, published by Indigo Dreams. Char loves honey almost as much as Winnie the Pooh, but feels sorry that bees get a raw deal from humans.

Jenny Morris is an award-winning writer of poems and fiction. Her latest poetry collection is *Lunatic Moon* (Gatehouse Press).

Hilary Murray, as a child, sitting on the back seat of her mother's car, was stung on the thigh by a bee. It was soon after this she began writing poetry. She used to buy clear wildflower honey in 7lb tubs, but these days finds a single jar sufficient.

Jo Peters is a retired teacher who now spends her time writing poetry, walking and botanising in the Yorkshire Dales and growing flowers for bees and butterflies. She has two friends who keep bees and delights in the gift of a pot of honey.

Caroline Price is a violinist and teacher living and working in Kent, where she also helps to run the Kent and Sussex Poetry Society. She has published three collections of poetry, the most recent being *Wishbone* (Shoestring Press 2008). She's interested in insects, and greatly concerned by the current plight of bees.

J A Priestman lives, works and writes in Oxfordshire, where friends keep bees who make extensive and alchemical use of her lavender borders.

Roz Quillan Chandler writes: 'At the moment life is mostly mixing poetry with designing my second wooden eco house. Sometimes a poem looks like a house or the design looks like a poem. I'm hoping they'll combine to become a happily creative place to live and work. I'll plant an orchard for the bees.'

Gina Shaw lives in Ilkley. She has had poems published in magazines and other Grey Hen publications. She has always been interested in nature and is especially fond of small creatures. Why bees? Honey for food; stings for arthritis; mystery; industry. Pollination – where would we be without them?

Penelope Shuttle's ninth collection, *Sandgrain and Hourglass* (Bloodaxe Books 2010) was a PBS Recommendation. *Unsent: New and Selected Poems* will be published by Bloodaxe in October 2012. Penelope shared Peter Redgrove's fascination with bees, and remembers with gladness the little bee brooch he bought her on a visit to a Cornish bee centre.

Pat Simmons grew up in London, but escaped as soon as she could, to Oxford and then Bristol. She was a copywriter with Oxfam and then head of communications for African development organisation Send a Cow. She was amazed to learn from beekeepers in Ghana that three beehives strategically placed can treble local crop yields.

Deborah Sloan squeezes poetry writing and flamenco dancing into the hours when she is not being a psychotherapeutic counsellor. Her affinity with bees stems, rather narcissistically, from the fact that

'Deborah' is Hebrew for 'bee'. Therefore she has a vested interest in doing her bit to help keep them from extinction.

Ruth Smith lives in Outer London and spends her time writing poems and travelling. When she writes she looks out onto a garden where she has planted herbs and all the flowers she can think of that will attract bees, including alpines. They still come but in much smaller numbers.

Margaret Speak has been widely published in magazines, has a pamphlet *The Firefly Cage* (Redbeck Press), and is a reviewer of poetry and fiction. She has won many prizes including Bridport, Cardiff, Mslexia and Torbay. She is coordinator of York Poetry Workshop and joint founder and organiser of the Yorkshire Open Poetry Competition.

Pauline Stainer is a freelance writer and tutor. After many years in rural Essex and then on the Orkney island of Rousay, she now lives in Suffolk. She has published seven collections, four of which were Poetry Book Society recommendations. 'The fact that *The Honeycomb* was my first published collection says it all!'

Sheila Templeton is an award-winning poet currently living in Glasgow. She has two poetry collections, *Slow Road Home* published by Makar Press (2004) and *Digging For Light* published by New Voices Press (2011). If deprived of her daily spoonful of honey, she becomes worryingly grumpy.

Isobel Thrilling was born in Suffolk, raised in Yorkshire, read English at Hull, worked as Head of ESL in London. She has a son, a daughter and two granddaughters. A prizewinner (Bridport and York), she has been widely published: magazines, anthologies, radio and television. Her latest book is *The Language Creatures* (Shearsman 2007).

Christine Webb has published two collections, *After Babel* (Peterloo 2004) and *Catching Your Breath* (Cinnamon Press 2011). Her interest in bees comes from beekeeping friends, as well as from a concern about the pollutant effect on bees of modern human behaviour.

Ann Williams is completing a D. Phil in Creative Writing at the University of Sussex, and has previously had work published in *Agenda*, *Resurgence*, *The London Magazine* and an anthology *Our Common Ground* (Silverdart 2011). Several recent poems contain a reference to bees, from an agricultural and historical perspective.

Sue Wood's poetry has appeared in numerous anthologies and journals. She won the Cinnamon Prize for poetry in 2008 followed by the publication of her first collection *Imagine yourself to be water* (Cinnamon Press 2009). She works as a freelance writer and tutor in and around Halifax, West Yorkshire, where she lives.

Liz Woods was born in East Yorkshire but now lives in Cornwall where she writes poetry and prose. She is currently working on her new book about Cornish food, history and folklore – including bees! *Cornish Feasts and Festivals* is due out from Alison Hodge Publishers in late 2012.

Lynne Wycherley writes: 'at depth, all my poetry is a kind of love poetry, whether for people or places, wild creatures or stars'. Her work has been widely published. Lynne's most recent book of poetry, *Poppy in a Storm-struck Field*, is available from Shoestring Press, Nottingham.

Index of Poets

Acknowledgements

ALISON BRACKENBURY 'Honeycomb' published in *Magma*. CAROLINE CARVER 'Dancing' published in *ARTEMISpoetry*. A C CLARKE 'May Swarm' published in *Weyfarers*. ROSE COOK 'Mother Hive' *Taking Flight* (Oversteps Books 2009). SALLY EVANS 'The Bees, Canto Four: Honey' The Bees (diehard 2008); 'The Honey Seller 1800' *The Honey Seller* (Firewater Press 2009). KATE FOLEY 'Beewoman' and 'Telling the Bees' *Soft Engineering* (Onlywomen Press 1994); ANGELA FRANCE 'Beeing' *Occupation* (Ragged Raven Press 2009). JOY HOWARD 'Honeysuckle' *Exit Moonshine* (Grey Hen Press 2009). ELEANOR LIVINGSTONE 'Golden' *Even the Sea* (Red Squirrel Press 2010). JENNY MORRIS 'Drone' *The Sin Eater* (NPF 1993). CAROLINE PRICE 'The Girls in the Miellerie' published in *The Rialto*; 'Figures of Eight' published in *Agenda*. SALLY EVANS 'The Bees, Canto Four: Honey' The Bees (diehard 2008); KATE FOLEY 'Beewoman' and 'Telling the Bees' *Soft Engineering* (Onlywomen Press 1994); ROZ QUILLAN CHANDLER 'Honey Guide' published in *Mslexia*; PAULINE STAINER 'Cargo' *The Honeycomb'* (Bloodaxe 1989); CHRISTINE WEBB 'Inch of Gold' *After Babel* (Peterloo Poets 2004). ANN WILLIAMS 'The Beekeeper ' published in *Resurgence* and *Our Common Ground* (Silverdart 2011); 'February', published in *The London Magazine*.

Joy Howard is the founder of Grey Hen Press, which specialises in publishing the work of older women poets. Her poems have featured in several anthologies: *Beautiful Barbarians* (Onlywomen 1986), *Dancing the Tightrope* (Women's Press 1987), *Naming the Waves* (Virago 1988), *Not for the Academy* (Onlywomen 1999), *The Argent Moon* (Pembrokeshire Press 2007), and *The Listening Shell* (Headland Press 2010). She has edited four previous Grey Hen Press anthologies, and published a collection of her own poems, *Exit Moonshine* (Grey Hen 2009) about her 'coming out' experiences in the 1980s. She has been published in *Sofia, Sphinx,* ARTEMIS*poetry, Lavender Review, The Interpreter's House* and *The Frogmore Papers.* Her poems can be found online at *Guardian Unlimited* and *poetry p f,* and feature in '*Poems While You Wait*' at St James's Hospital in Leeds. A new collection, *Refurbishment,* was published by Ward Wood in 2011.